D0843209

new seasons®

New Seasons is a registered trademark of Publications International, Ltd.

Written by Brandon Myers

Photography from: Shutterstock.com

Louis Weber, CEO
Publications International, Ltd.
8140 Lehigh Avenue
Morton Grove, IL 60053

www.pilbooks.com

8 7 6 5 4 3 2 1

ISBN: 978-1-64558-373-8

Let's get social!

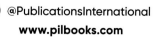 @Publications_International

@PublicationsInternational

www.pilbooks.com

PUPPIES IN PAJAMAS

You stole all the covers!

6

I was hoping for something
a little more outdoorsy.

I could really use a hug.

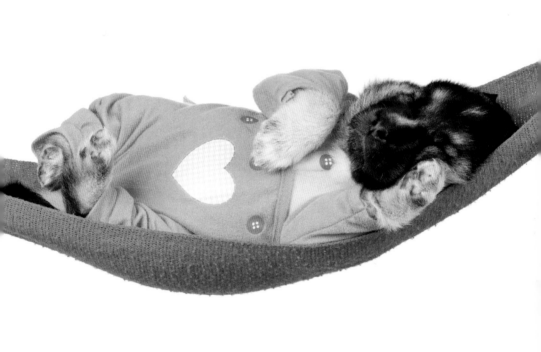

Yeah, I got the hint—sleep like a baby.

When is bedtime again?
I was only half-paying attention.

My ears were cold.

Teddy is sad you didn't
buy him matching pajamas.

Hopefully the cat won't even see me tonight.

Oh, are you sleeping up there on my bed tonight too?

My heart is on my sleeve,
and my happies are in my tail.

You can turn off the lights,
but you can't turn off the wiggles.

For sleep, I prefer boxers to briefs.

We know it's quiet time—it's the PJs that are so loud.

Why do you keep calling me Nighty Night?

I keep dreaming of pulling
a big sled full of toys and treats.

Listen, I already told you
it's not a doll. It's a sleep aid.

Every day should be pajama day.

Don't worry. Chihuahuasaurus
will guard you tonight.

The mysterious crashing sounds
you are about to hear are intended
for a sleeping audience only.

Tomorrow is Sunday. I can sleep in, right?

Fine, I'll sleep in it. But I'm not going for walkies dressed like this.

You may have hidden my pillow
in the laundry basket but I found it
and you're not taking it again.

They say follow your dream.

Well, my dream is to be a space unicorn.

I don't always bark at night, but when I do,
it's for absolutely no reason.

Shh, I'm dreaming of a big fish dinner.

I tried to hit the sack, but the sack ate me.

Ted is zonked.

Help us carry him to bed.

I find your idea of baths
before bedtime totally quackers.

Good night, Moon.

I have no off button but I might
have a temporary sleep mode.

I see you've put on your jammies too.

I have to go outside.

I heart sleepytimes!

G'night little buddy.

If you think I'm sleeping in the garage again, you're in for a very loud night.

You've heard Three Dog Night, but what about Three Bulldogs Snoring?

Can't tell which one is puppy
and which one is teddy, can you?

You don't understand.
Dogs can't sleep on the bed—
unicorns are fine.

Admit it: you think I'm cute even when I'm snoring.

You can turn out the lights,
but you can't turn off my ears.

Stretches, squirrel chasing, squeaky toy calisthenics . . . I'm beat!

A hot shower, warm robe, and I'm done for the day.

A couple of disco naps and we'll be on our way.

If you call me Santa Claws one more time . . .

Why do I keep dreaming
I'm in the Boston Marathon?

Nothing like turning in early
on a cold winter's night.

The morning began quietly, but soon turned into a dog's breakfast.

When you have a minute, could you write "I'm with stupid" on this?

I hear crinkling. Midnight snack?

Let's compromise: you let me sleep in bed,
and I won't bark all night.

Is anybunny getting sleepy?

You say I'm spoiled like it's a bad thing.

Well, you said we would be sleeping on a water bed.